CODE RED
MARCH 25, 1911

The Triangle Shirtwaist Factory Fire

by Jacqueline Dembar Greene

Consultant: David Von Drehle
Author of *Triangle: The Fire That Changed America*

BEARPORT
PUBLISHING

New York, New York

Credits

Cover and Title Page, © Keystone/Getty Images; 3, © UNITE HERE Archives, Kheel Center, Cornell University; 4, © Brown Brothers; 5, Courtesy Library of Congress Prints and Photographs Division; 6, © The Granger Collection, New York; 8L, Courtesy Library of Congress Prints and Photographs Division; 8R, © Culver Pictures; 9, © Bettmann/CORBIS; 10, © Brown Brothers; 11, © UNITE HERE Archives, Kheel Center, Cornell University; 12-13, © UNITE HERE Archives, Kheel Center, Cornell University; 14, Courtesy Library of Congress Prints and Photographs Division; 15, © Brown Brothers; 16, © Brown Brothers; 17, © UNITE HERE Archives, Kheel Center, Cornell University; 18, © UNITE HERE Archives, Kheel Center, Cornell University; 19, © Brown Brothers; 20-21, © Brown Brothers; 22, © UNITE HERE Archives, Kheel Center, Cornell University; 23, Courtesy Library of Congress Prints and Photographs Division; 24, © UNITE HERE Archives, Kheel Center, Cornell University; 25, © UNITE HERE Archives, Kheel Center, Cornell University; 26-27, © UNITE HERE Archives, Kheel Center, Cornell University; 28T, © UNITE HERE Archives, Kheel Center, Cornell University; 28B, © UNITE HERE Archives, Kheel Center, Cornell University; 29T, © Brown Brothers; 29B, © Hadwin Collection, Kheel Center, Cornell University; 29 Background, © The Granger Collection, New York; 30, © UNITE HERE Archives, Kheel Center, Cornell University; 31, © UNITE HERE Archives, Kheel Center, Cornell University.

Publisher: Kenn Goin
Editorial Director: Adam Siegel
Creative Director: Spencer Brinker
Photo Researcher: Beaura Kathy Ringrose
Design: Dawn Beard Creative

Library of Congress Cataloging-in-Publication Data

Greene, Jacqueline Dembar.
  The Triangle Shirtwaist Factory fire / by Jacqueline Dembar Greene ; consultant, David Von Drehle.
    p. cm. — (Code red)
  Includes bibliographical references and index.
  ISBN-13: 978-1-59716-359-0 (library binding)
  ISBN-10: 1-59716-359-7 (library binding)
  1. Triangle Shirtwaist Company—Fire, 1911—Juvenile literature. 2. New York (N.Y.)—History—1898–1951—Juvenile literature. 3. Clothing factories—New York (State)—New York—Safety measures—History—20th century—Juvenile literature. 4. Labor laws and legislation—New York (State)—New York—History—20th century—Juvenile literature. I. Von Drehle, Dave. II. Title.

  F128.5.G785 2007
  974.7'041—dc22

                    2006026707

For more information, write to Bearport Publishing Company, Inc., 101 Fifth Avenue, Suite 6R, New York, New York 10003. Printed in the United States of America.

10 9 8 7 6 5 4 3 2

Contents

Fire!

It was late afternoon on Saturday, March 25, 1911. At the Triangle Waist Company in New York City, factory workers were finishing their day. All week long they had cut and **stitched** pieces of cloth to make **shirtwaists**. Soon they could collect their pay and go home. On Sunday, they could rest.

Sewing rooms in factories were often crowded with workers and cloth.

Suddenly, Eva Harris ran across the workroom on the eighth floor. She squeezed past tables piled with cotton cloth. "Fire!" she shouted. Samuel Bernstein, the manager, saw smoky flames near the cutting tables. Workers grabbed buckets filled with water.

In the early 1900s, women wore long skirts and blouses called shirtwaists.

About 500 people worked at the Triangle factory the day of the fire. Most were women. Many were Italian or Jewish **immigrants**. Some were as young as 14 years old.

Where Is the Water?

Workmen threw buckets of water on the flames, but the fire raced across the room. Huge bins of cloth scraps hadn't been emptied for weeks. The cloth burst into flames.

The men pulled a fire hose from the wall. Samuel Bernstein turned the nozzle, but nothing came out.

"Where is the water?" he cried.

The Triangle Waist Company took up the top three floors of the Asch Building. At ten floors, the building was one of New York City's new **skyscrapers**.

The Asch Building

Women tried to get out. Flames blocked one of the doors. So workers ran to the second door—but it was locked! They screamed, beating the locked door with their fists. A factory worker, Louis Brown, pushed the women aside. Using a key, he was able to open the door. Workers streamed down the stairs.

66 Flames were already blazing fiercely and spreading fast. If we couldn't get out we would all be roasted alive. 99

–Rosie Safran, factory worker

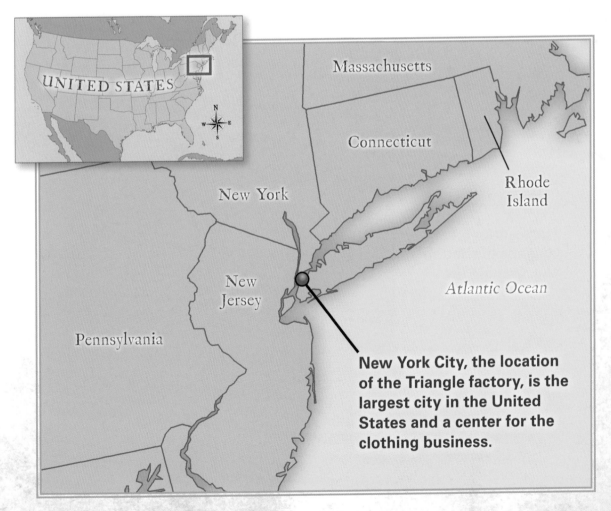

New York City, the location of the Triangle factory, is the largest city in the United States and a center for the clothing business.

Sound the Alarm

When the fire started, Dinah Lipschitz was handing out pay envelopes on the eighth floor. She grabbed the telephone and alerted the factory owners on the tenth floor. On the street, a person rushed to a fire alarm box and pulled the lever. Soon fire engines raced to the building.

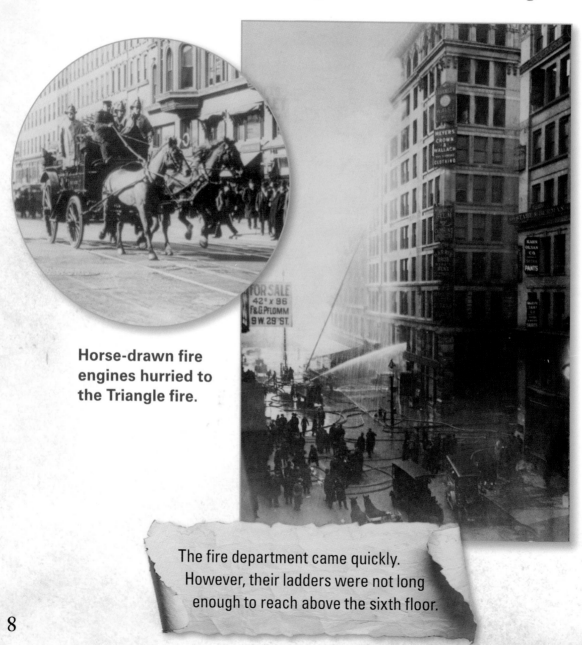

Horse-drawn fire engines hurried to the Triangle fire.

The fire department came quickly. However, their ladders were not long enough to reach above the sixth floor.

Windows in the building exploded from the heat. Fire leaped into the **stairwells**. Workers on the tenth floor dashed through the smoke and flames to the roof. Their hair and clothes were burned. The owners got to the roof, too. Students in a taller building next door set up ladders between the buildings' roofs. They helped dozens climb to safety.

> **66** The only way for you to get out is the roof! **99**
>
> —Samuel Bernstein, shouting to frightened people on the tenth floor

Workers jammed into the building's two tiny elevator cars. The roof of this elevator collapsed when workers who couldn't get inside jumped down the shaft and landed on top of the car.

9

Escape!

Panicked workers rushed to the windows. They crowded onto a narrow fire escape. It didn't reach all the way to the ground, but at least it would lead them farther from the flames.

From the fire escape, one woman smashed in a window on the sixth floor. A few workers climbed inside. Then, without warning, the fire escape broke. Many people fell to their deaths.

The fire escape was too weak to hold more than a few people at a time. The weight of the escaping workers caused it to collapse.

66 I still had one foot on the fire escape... People were falling all around me, screaming all around me. The fire escape was collapsing. **99**

–Abe Gordon, sewing machine repairman, who climbed from the fire escape through the sixth-floor window

About 200 workers were trapped on the ninth floor. Smoke choked them. Flames burned at their feet. On the sidewalk below, firemen held **safety nets**.

One woman jumped, then more, but the nets were not strong enough. Jumpers crashed right through them and hit the pavement.

Police stand near the bodies of several workers who jumped from the burning building.

There had been four small fires in the Asch Building the year before. The owners didn't try to make the building safer, however. They claimed it was **fireproof**.

Flying Bundles

Workers still trapped inside saw that the safety nets wouldn't save them. They still decided to jump rather than burn in the fire. Some held hands, stepped off the window ledge, and fell together.

One young couple kissed each other goodbye. The man dropped his sweetheart over the edge. Then he stepped through the window and jumped.

A large crowd of people rushed to the area. They heard about the Triangle fire and were searching for family members and friends.

On the street below, people thought **bundles** of burning cloth were flying through the air. Then they realized the bundles were young women. They watched with horror as the bodies landed.

None of the workers who jumped survived. The few who were taken alive to the hospital soon died from their injuries.

Finding Their Families

In about 30 minutes, firefighters were able to get the fire under control. Smoke and ash filled the air. Hundreds of workers had somehow managed to escape. Yet 146 people had died. Burned bodies covered the ninth floor of the Triangle factory. Others lay lifeless on the sidewalk.

66 This is the worst I ever saw. **99**

–New York City police officer, who saw the dead bodies from inside the building being placed on the sidewalk

Bodies were placed in wooden coffins and brought to a large building near the East River.

City workers brought wooden **coffins** for the dead. Wagons carried them to a **gloomy** building called Misery Lane.

Shocked relatives formed a sad line outside Misery Lane. It stretched along the street. People had to find their daughters or sons, sisters or brothers, husbands or wives. Somehow, they had to identify them.

Of the 146 people who died in the Triangle fire, 123 were women.

Some bodies were burned so badly, their families could recognize them only by a ring or other jewelry.

15

Workers on Strike

When firefighters had been racing to the Triangle factory, Frances Perkins had also hurried to the building. Perkins had worked hard to make conditions safer for factory workers.

Standing on the sidewalk, Perkins watched the falling bodies. She promised herself she would do whatever she could to keep another **disaster** like this from happening again.

Frances Perkins

❝I shall never forget the frozen horror which came over us as we stood with our hands on our throats watching that horrible sight, knowing that there was no help.❞

–Frances Perkins, recalling the sight of workers jumping

Perkins believed that workers should form **labor unions**. She thought that by banding together, workers could win better conditions and higher pay.

Just two years before the Triangle fire, in 1909, clothing workers went on **strike**. Most factories finally agreed to make life better for workers. The Triangle factory owners, however, refused.

More than 20,000 workers, most of them women, went on strike against the clothing industry in 1909. It was one of the largest strikes of the time.

All Work, Little Pay

In the early 1900s, clothing factories were crowded and noisy. People worked 12 or even 14 hours a day, 6 days a week. Sometimes they had to pay a **fine** if they came late. They often worked behind locked doors.

Workers got paid only for clothing pieces they finished. So they had to work fast. Sometimes they were charged for the electricity, needles, and thread that they used.

Rose Schneiderman was a clothing worker and union leader. She once said, "I know from experience it is up to the working people to save themselves."

Sewing machine workers earned between $8 and $13 each week. It wasn't always enough to pay for food, rent, and medical care.

Why did people work in factories when conditions were so terrible? It was hard for immigrants to get better jobs. Many didn't speak English well. Their families were poor. Even low-paying jobs helped buy food.

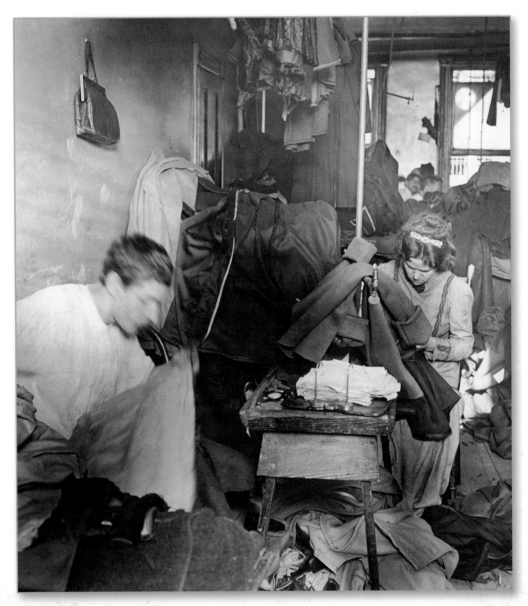

Many immigrants were forced to work in tiny, crowded factories, called sweatshops.

What Went Wrong?

The Triangle Waist Company was in a modern building that was only ten years old. It was built to be fireproof.

After the terrible fire was over, officials found that the building itself was still in good shape. Only the cloth, machines, and wooden parts of the windows and doors had burned.

The fire at the Triangle factory didn't destroy the building. However, everything inside the workrooms was burned.

So many people died because the factory had ignored important safety rules. Long tables and boxes blocked the exits. Fire hoses did not work properly. The fire escape was too narrow and didn't reach the street. Stairways were also not wide enough. Worst of all were the locked doors that trapped workers inside.

At the time of the Triangle fire, it was against the law to keep doors locked while people were working.

Who Is to Blame?

The Triangle fire probably started when a worker broke the "no smoking" rule and dropped a cigarette or hot match. Still, many New Yorkers blamed the factory owners. They hadn't followed fire safety laws.

People were especially angry about the locked doors. They believed that if the doors had not been locked, many more workers would have survived.

The Triangle Waist Company owners, Max Blanck (left) and Isaac Harris (right), had built a successful business. They were called "the Shirtwaist Kings."

Max Blanck and Isaac Harris owned the Triangle Waist Company. Most people thought they should be punished. The city brought them to court. A **jury** listened to the facts. In the end, it decided there wasn't enough proof that the owners were to blame for the deaths. The jury voted "not guilty."

" Murderers! Not guilty? Not guilty? Where is the justice? "
–David Weiner, brother of a fire victim, shouting at Blanck and Harris as they left the court

During the trial, worker Kate Alterman sobbed as she described the fire to the jury.

After the trial, several families sued Blanck and Harris. Eventually each of these families received just $75 for the deaths of their loved ones.

Demanding Change

On April 5, 1911, a huge march of 120,000 workers **protested** unsafe conditions that caused the Triangle fire. More than 400,000 New Yorkers lined the streets to support them. "A similar tragedy must never take place in New York again," one protestor said.

New Yorkers filled the streets and marched beside the coffins of fire victims.

New York State leaders agreed that changes were needed. They set up a **commission** to study ways to make factories safer. They required all tall buildings to have **sprinkler systems**.

People throughout the country also reacted to the terror of the fire. Towns, cities, and states passed new laws. Workplaces had to hold fire drills. They had to keep hallways clear and doors unlocked.

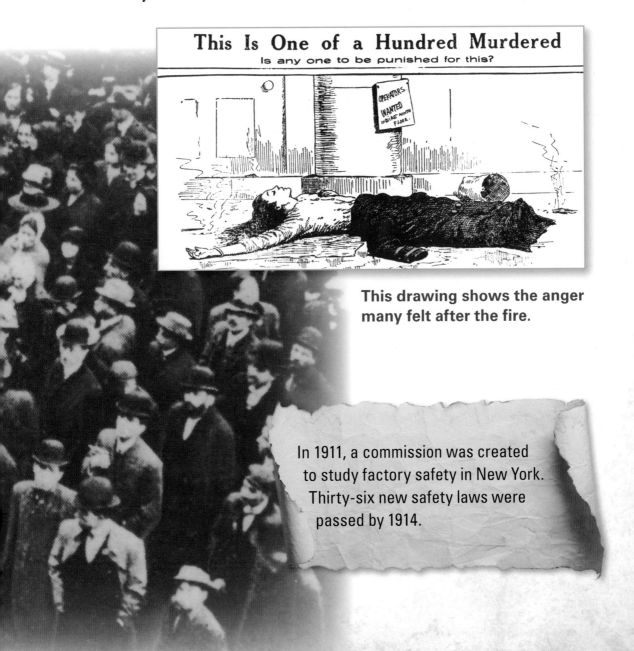

This Is One of a Hundred Murdered

Is any one to be punished for this?

OPERATORS WANTED INQUIRE NINTH FLOOR.

This drawing shows the anger many felt after the fire.

In 1911, a commission was created to study factory safety in New York. Thirty-six new safety laws were passed by 1914.

Remembering a Tragedy

Too many workers lost their lives in the Triangle fire. Yet the disaster led many Americans to fight for change. People joined together to make factories better, and safer, places to work.

In 1961, 50 years after the disaster, crowds gathered in New York City to remember the victims of the Triangle fire.

Today, fire safety codes are very strict. Businesses and factories have smoke alarms, fireproof stairways, and sprinkler systems. Fire departments are amazingly fast and skilled at rescuing people.

The workers at the Triangle factory died around 100 years ago. Yet the improved working conditions that resulted from their tragedy are still keeping people safe today.

"They did not die in vain and we will never forget them."
—Frances Perkins, speaking at the 50th anniversary of the Triangle fire

Profiles

Many people played an important role in the events connected to the Triangle fire. Here are five of them.

Max Blanck and Isaac Harris were the owners of the Triangle Waist Company.

- Were Russian immigrants
- Worked in small clothing shops before starting the Triangle Waist Company
- Had hundreds of workers at electric sewing machines in their factory
- Opened a new factory together after the fire, which went out of business a few years later

Clara Lemlich was a leader of the 1909 strike against the clothing industry.

- Was an immigrant from the Ukraine
- Came to the United States at age 17
- Worked in a clothing factory, where she thought owners treated workers like machines
- Was beaten and arrested but kept fighting for workers to get higher pay, fewer hours, and safer jobs

Frances Perkins never worked in a factory—but fought to help those who did.

- Was one of the few women of her time to attend college
- Helplessly watched women jump to their deaths during the Triangle fire
- Hired by the government of New York to improve working conditions
- Named the first secretary of labor by President Franklin D. Roosevelt in 1933

Joseph Zito was an elevator operator in the Asch Building.

- Tried to save as many people as possible when fire broke out in the Triangle factory
- Went through flames and smoke to save workers until the elevator became stuck under the bodies of women who had jumped on top of it
- Along with another elevator operator, helped save 150 people

Glossary

bundles (BUHN-duhlz) groups of things that have been wrapped, tied, or fastened together

coffins (KAWF-inz) containers in which dead people are placed for burying

commission (kuh-MISH-in) a group of people working together to study a problem

disaster (duh-ZASS-tur) an event causing much damage, loss, or suffering

fine (FINE) money that is paid as a punishment

fireproof (FIRE-*proof*) unable to be burned

gloomy (GLOO-mee) filled with sadness

immigrants (IM-uh-gruhnts) people who travel to a country to live and make their homes

jury (JU-ree) a group of people that listens to facts at a trial and makes a decision about who is to blame

labor unions (LAY-bur YOON-yuhnz) organizations made up of workers who are trying to protect or improve their working conditions, such as their pay or the number of hours per week that they must work

panicked (PAN-ikt) terrified; filled with fear

protested (pruh-TEST-id) expressed disagreement

safety nets (SAYF-tee NETS) large, strong nets that are made to catch people who fall or jump from high in the air

shirtwaists (SHURT-waysts) loose shirts, or blouses, for women

skyscrapers (SKYE-*skray*-purz) very tall buildings

sprinkler systems (SPRINGK-lur SISS-tuhmz) water pipes that spray water; in a building they are used to put out fires

stairwells (STAIR-welz) the parts of a building where stairs are located

stitched (STICHT) sewn

strike (STRIKE) stopped working in order to force an employer to change working conditions

Bibliography

Burns, Ric, and James Sanders, with Lisa Ades. *New York: An Illustrated History.* New York: Knopf (1999).

Goodman, Edward C. *Fire!: The 100 Most Devastating Fires and the Heroes Who Fought Them.* New York: Black Dog & Leventhal (2001).

Malkiel, Theresa S. *The Diary of a Shirtwaist Striker.* Ithaca, NY: ILR Press, Cornell University (1990).

Von Drehle, David. *Triangle: The Fire That Changed America.* New York: Atlantic Monthly Press (2003).

Read More

Landau, Elaine. *Fires.* New York: Franklin Watts (1999).

Schaefer, A.R. *The Triangle Shirtwaist Factory Fire.* Milwaukee, WI: World Almanac Library (2003).

Sherrow, Victoria. *The Triangle Factory Fire.* Brookfield, CT: Millbrook Press (1995).

Learn More Online

To learn more about the Triangle factory fire, visit:
www.bearportpublishing.com/CodeRed

Index

About the Author

Jacqueline Dembar Greene is an award-winning author of more than 20 fiction and nonfiction books and stories, including *The 2001 World Trade Center Attack*. She has illustrated some of her nonfiction books with original photographs. Learn more at www.jdgbooks.com.